Preface

I have been fortunate to have lived through a time in history in America to have seen some of the most significant changes in technology and social issues that have ever occurred in this country and in the world.

In my adolescent years there was no television or computers and few electrical appliances.
In those times everyone knew their neighbors and helped each other out in times of need.
People would gather on the weekends for ball games, picnics and just for socializing.

The first change that would change America forever was the television. As more and more people got a TV they would socialize less and less until after a few years no one visited their neighbors anymore or even knew who their new neighbors were.

In the post WWII years and into the 50's and 60's in the political world there was little talk about liberals or conservatives or the "left" or "right'.

It appeared that the majority of reporters were more independent in their reporting of the news and no political bias was apparent by the radio and TV news people or in the newspapers. Politicians were only identified as a Democrat or Republican.

Another major change in America was the health care system. Prior to the late 50's and early 60's nearly every family had a private insurance plan and the rates were affordable. For those who did not carry insurance, if they had a medical problem they could work out an affordable payment plan with the doctor or hospital or the community would chip in to help out. In the late 50's major corporations began to offer health insurance plans to their employees as a method to secure and keep good employees. Naturally all of the major companies followed suit and by the 70's most major companies with a significant employee base offered health insurance for their employees. What that did was cause the health care costs and insurance premiums to start escalating out of control to be the mess it is today.

The insurance companies had a captive base of customers with the employers and when the insurance rates got higher, so did the health care providers' cost to the insurance carriers and then employers were forced to charge the employees a copay for the premiums. Today, employees are now rebelling against higher co-pays and some employers are dropping their health insurance coverage altogether.

Another major thing I have witnessed over the past 50 years is the development of many technologies never dreamed of before. I saw the first landing on the moon and I was in Silicon Valley when the first microprocessor was invented. These are all good things for Americans and mankind throughout the world.

The most disappointing thing for me is what this country has become in terms of being disunited, and the greed and corruption, especially within our public entities. I fear the post baby boomer generations may never see how great America was, prior to 40 years ago.

It is the condition that America is in now that compels me to speak out about some of the things I find wrong and to offer some of my common sense solutions.

Contents

Voters

Voters execute a curious dichotomy between their desire for change in the country's direction and to elect different individuals to represent them in government. They get excited during election primary seasons but then they don't show up at the polls to vote.

There has always been a propensity for the voters to re-elect the same people over and over again while at the same time wanting a different result. They see a name they may recognize and just vote for the incumbents again without checking any other candidates who maybe will do a better job for them. Especially in recent years, a large number of the voters vote only along party lines and ignore what the candidates have done or what they stand for. This is a total abdication of the voter's responsibility to elect the candidate which will serve the voters the best, because the politicians directly affect our lives in terms of taxes we pay and regulations we must live with in our daily lives.

(1)

Voters have a tenancy to downplay the primary elections and wait for the general election but that is too late to make a change. The primary election is the most important time to make a change of office holders and also the most important time to vote to insure they make it to the general election.

One huge problem with voters is they give too much credence to the office of Governor and President. The Governors and President do not make legislation or laws. They can only suggest what they want, but the Legislature is the body that enacts laws. Therefore, the state and federal representatives is where all the emphasis should be placed.

The voters need to pay attention to the record and backgrounds of those running for office. In a TV interview with Chris Wallace on 2/13/11, Mississippi Governor Haley Barbour was asked what makes him unique versus the other potential Republican candidates who may run and he said because he had been a lobbyist, politician and a lawyer and that was

the perfect trifecta for any political candidate's qualifications.

Are you kidding me? That's exactly the kind of people we don't need in office. A lobbyist will lobby for anything for the right price, the politician will take contributions from anyone and if elected will repay them by way of a tax break or regulatory measure in their favor or an earmark for their company or state and finally a lawyer is all about the art of illusion and creating a perception in order to win cases for their client: in this case, his or her contributors and constituents.

As a general rule, lawyers and educators don't make good politicians because they have no exposure or background with the real world private sector. Yet these individuals make up more than 60% of our political institutions.

Most politicians start at the local level then make their way up the political ladder by running for a state office and then make their way into Congress. Thus, they should be

scrutinized closely by the voters at their lowest level and if they are not performing in the interests of the taxpayers, they should be voted out then. Voters are very complacent when it comes to following the track records of people in office. They are susceptible to name recognition or the politicians' status in the community. The voters need to follow the politicians' performance at the city and county levels and weed out the bad public servants then before they get to a more prominent level at the state or federal level.

Voters tend to think that city officials and County supervisors are only there to look out for their interests but these officials can have a direct effect on your pocket books with fees on your utilities, parking, admission to parks and recreation, taxes on your home and business licenses and fees. With the deficit condition of cities, counties and states today, it seems like the politicians only wish to spend more money and bring in more revenue from the taxpayers to pay for their overspending.

(4)

Politicians cannot even be honest in how they
portray their ballet propositions. They headline
a proposition one way, but in the detail it may
mean something completely different. The
voters don't take the time to read the details
and simply vote on what they think it is about.
An example was California Proposition 28
which was titled "Limits on Legislators' Terms
In Office". "Limits the time a person may serve
in the Legislature from 14 to 12 years".
It passed by a landslide, leaving the voters to
believe they had actually reduced term limits.
Is that what it really was? Well, not exactly.
It actually increased the time in the Assembly
from 6 to 12 years and the time in the Senate
from 8 to 12 years. The 14 came from the fact
that they could be in one house for 6 then the
other for 8 but now they have added 6 years
to one house and 4 to the other, thus extending
term limits in both houses.

In summary, everyone should spend a few
hours reading the details of their propositions
and investigating their political candidates
and their records, which can be easily done

with the information available on the internet
and then make sure to vote well informed in
the primary and general elections with high
emphasis on the primary election.

Congress

Politicians want us to believe that they want to hold office to do the right thing for their constituents at home and for the good of the country and some earnestly do, but when they get in office, it seems the only interest they have is self-interest for a long-lasting and lucrative career. After all, where can you work in the private sector and get the job benefits that are given the members of Congress.

How many times have we heard of a member of Congress who was making $100-$200K in the private sector and after 3-5 years in Congress, they are worth millions. How does that happen? Could they have acquired wealth because of the lobbyists or special interest people and companies they supported?

Because of the economy and jobs situation in the past few years, the American people are beginning to look closer at what's going on in Washington and they are getting an eye full. The politicians believe the people are too ignorant

(7)

or are not paying attention to what they say and do, but the internet and various advocacy groups for better government have shined the light on them.

In theory it would seem that opposing parties could discuss the pros and cons of proposed legislation, reach compromise and enact bills that truly benefit the country as a whole but in practice all they do is take sides based on their ideology and get very little done.

When bills are discussed on the Senate or House floor, countless hours and days are wasted by the members orating on non-related subjects or chastising the opposing party for their alleged views. Members will speak in lock step with the party leaders agenda and rarely exhibit an original thought of their own. One need only watch C-SPAN or C-SPAN2 to see this shameful behavior and waste of the taxpayer's representation dollars.

The process of assembling and passing bills is totally flawed. Bills with a primary purpose

end up with unrelated items in it and/or pork unrelated to the bill. This practice is used to buy opposing votes for the main bill. This is Congress's idea of compromise. This is how the American people get fooled and find out later about things they never would have approved of if the additions to a bill had been disclosed in the open.

When the public finds out about such things as the "bridge to nowhere" or a 2 million dollar crossing for turtles or a 7 million renovation to a rural airport that only has 2 flights a day, they are shocked and surprised that could happen, but it was all there in the details. The famous statement regarding the Health Care bill by Speaker Pelosi when she said "we need to hurry up and pass the bill so we can find out what's in it" says it all.

A rule needs to be put in the Senate and the House that requires every bill to contain only material directly related to it to be included. Unrelated items to a bill and requests for pork should be submitted separately on their own

(9)

bill so that the members and the public can see what is trying to be passed or spent and can be discussed on their own merits.

Politicians use friendly or politically correct terms when talking about spending taxpayer money like the word "invest". To a private sector person the term "invest" implies you are investing discretionary funds in the stock market or a business but the politician means "spend" taxpayer dollars. When the term "cut" is used, it really means a reduction in the budget amount in the future and not a cut to what they are currently spending.

If there was a program or entitlement in the prior year for $10 billion and they want an increase of $2 billion in the current year, then say they are going to cut that program by 20% which would be $2.4 billion ($10B + $2B x 20%) but what they really mean is 20% of the $2 billion increase or $400 million so now the new total to spend is $11.6 billion and they have not cut anything, but in fact increased what they will spend by $1.6 billion.

(10)

When a new entitlement bill is submitted to Congress, the two parties will argue over how it is to be paid for, usually resulting in two alternatives: raise taxes or cut spending in an existing program. In either case, the proposed solution is usually to take effect in the future year or years after the current election cycle so that campaigning members don't have to justify it to their constituents until after they are re-elected. Promising to cut something in the future is a non-binding and dishonest tactic because future Congress's have no obligation to honor it.

In the private sector when a business is going to enter into a new venture, they do a R.O.I. (return on investment) analysis to figure out the total cost against the estimated revenues to see if it is going to be a profitable undertaking.

When government starts a program where they are going to be paying out money, they only estimate the amount of money they will be paying out and try to find a method (taxes or cuts) to pay for it but they do not factor in the

costs of implementing the program. After the bill has passed, agencies are set up all over the country with office leases, administration, oversight and enforcement personnel with no limits or oversight on the process and it then continues to grow, year after year.

Congress as well as all government employees should have to participate in Social Security, health insurance and pension plans the same as people in the private sector do. Maybe then they can see how it is to live with the rules they make. A retired or member voted out should not get a pension and health care for the rest of their lives. It should end with them leaving Washington and should never be for more than they earned while in office.

It seems the makeup of Congress follows the old "80/20" rule whereby 20% of the members are honest and truly try to do the right things for our country and 80% are there for their own self-serving interests and are a waste of the taxpayer's money.

(12)

Currently Senators are elected for 6 year terms and Representatives are elected for 2 year terms but there is no limit on how many times they can run for re-election. The supreme court ruled in 1995 (U.S. Term Limits, Inc. v Thornton) that any change must be done via a constitutional amendment. A change is needed to keep Congress fresh with new ideas and that should be done, along with the balanced budget amendment.

It seems to be a waste of time and a lot of money to have Representative elections every 2 years. New members spend the first year getting acclimated to the House and then half of the second year trying to get re-elected. A term of 4 years seems more reasonable with a life-time limit of 2 terms or 8 years.

A Senate term of 6 years is reasonable but there should be a limit of 2 life-time terms. The combined limit of terms in the Senate and the House should also be 2 terms per life-time. A House member serving one term could run for one term in the Senate or a Senator having

served one term in the Senate could run for one additional term in the House.

Political Contributions

A major breach to the integrity and honesty in politics in America is the ability of entities or individuals outside government who have the relationships to the government to influence the office holders to serve their interests in return for political contributions. This existing egregious policy is an obvious open invitation for corruption and fraud at all levels of government.

It is inherently immoral for a public office holder to accept contributions from individuals or companies who will benefit from their relationship to the government.
Government officials will support laws or regulations which clearly are not in accords with the wishes of the people and it is all due to the practice of rewarding contributors for their contributions to keep the officials in office.

In order to prevent the temptation or actual

(15)

practice of corruption by public employees, a law should be enacted that prohibits public employees from receiving contributions from anyone who does business with the government. Any organization or individual who receives public funds or public employee funds should not be allowed to contribute to any public employees or political candidates who may become public employees if elected. This includes unions representing public employees and all organizations partially or fully supported by public funds, such as the NEA.

Public schools (primarily universities and colleges) should not be allowed to contribute to individuals or PACs (political action committees) or national political groups since they are supported by taxpayer dollars. Even if this were legal, the taxpayers have no choice in who will receive the donations. It is hard to comprehend how our public schools can donate so much money to politicians when they are all in the red.

(16)

In the years 2009 and 2010, $120 million was paid by our public schools to politicians with nearly 90% going to the Democrat National Committee (DNC) or Democrat individuals running for re-election. From January through the first week of February in 2012, $3.4 million was donated by public schools at a time they were having trouble paying teachers and raising the student tuition at campuses all across the country. Does that make any sense at all?

Since 2012 is expected to be a high-cost election year, could the average 30% tuition raise that occurred during the fourth quarter of 2011 have a connection to the anticipated higher donations the schools will be asked to contribute?

In summary, contributions to public employees and political candidates vying to be employees, whether they be money or in-kind, should be prohibited by any individual or any organization that has a relationship to the government and all government entities such

(17)

as schools, should be prohibited from making contributions to political candidates using the taxpayer's money.

Judges

The only area of the constitution that our forefathers didn't cover well is our Judges with respect to how they hold office and their tenures on the bench. For district and supreme court justices, the President appoints a judge and then they are ratified by the Senate. At the state level, some states allow the Governor to appoint judges and some have commissions that vet the candidates and then have them appointed by the governor. This allows a political party in power to fill the benches with judges who are of the same ideology.

The duty of judges is to insure that issues that come before them are judged against the laws in effect and whether or not they are constitutional, not to rewrite the constitution or circumvent the laws of the land.
It is not their duty to interpret or change the law to try to impose their personal desires.

One of the worst fallacies of the legal system is the use of "precedence". Every time a case is

(19)

tried, the first thing the lawyers do is look to prior cases of relevance in order to support their position on the case. The problem with that is, that if a similar case has been tried and the judge took liberties in rendering judgment which is contrary to the law of the land or does not agree with the constitution, a bad precedence can be carried forward indefinitely.

The most important thing in the judicial system is to have judges with integrity who will follow the laws and the constitution. In order to make sure we get the best judges possible, they should not be appointed by one individual or political party. All district, appeals and supreme court judges should be elected by the people. This will insure we get the best judges on the bench for the most important issues of the land. If we allow ideology or politics to enter the judicial system, then the integrity of the system is in jeopardy.

The nominations for a seat at the state or federal court levels should be made by congress where each party (Democrat,

(20)

Republican and all other parties) can nominate up to two candidates to a maximum of six and then they will go on the next election ballot. If there is a vacancy on any bench due to death or resignation, then the governor or the president can appoint a judge subject to confirmation by the state or federal legislature but their tenure would only be until the next election.

To insure we have the keenest minds on the bench at all times there should be term limits and age limits. A maximum term on the bench should be 15 years or attainment of age 75, whichever comes first. No matter how brilliant some of the judges are or have been, they are subject to the same ills of age that befall all of us, such as dementia.

One in three people over the age of 65 will suffer dementia. We have all seen it with our parents and grandparents so how can we think that all the justices on the supreme court or any court for that matter, be immune from it. We currently have five justices on the supreme

court who are over 65 with four of those approaching 80, so it is not a stretch to think that at least two may be suffering from dementia.

In summary, we need to elect the most important judges in the land and keep the benches fresh with intellect and remove the political appointments and influence out of our judicial system.

Entitlements

First of all, the term "entitlements" is misused when referring to all the various programs employed by the Federal and State governments. The constitution does not grant anyone an entitlement for any reason. The only programs that are entitlements are the Social Security and Medicare systems, and that is only by virtue of the fact that the taxpayer and their employer paid for it and therefore they are entitled to collect them. All other programs are give away programs but for purpose of discussion I refer to them all as entitlements.

The following are some of the government programs that are in use:

Medicare
This fund is for medical care for those who have reached the age of 65 and is paid for by contributions from the employee and employer. From 1966 until 1993 there were annual limits for paying into Medicare, with the last limit being when wages reached $135,000, but since

1993 there is no wage limit. It covers 80% of doctors and hospital bills at health providers that accept Medicare. If a person retires early or at any age between 62 and 65, they do not qualify for Medicare until they reach age 65.

Supplemental Security Income (SSI)
This is for the blind and disabled people who have mental or physical disabilities that last or are expected to last 12 months or more and is funded by income taxes from the general fund. There is no coverage for dependents.

While the Supplemental Security Income program is certainly worthy for the blind and certain disabilities, it also includes disabilities which are questionable and controllable by some who qualified to be on the program, an overweight condition, for example.
Health services and drugs for people on this program is handled by the Medicaid system in each state.

Social Security Disability Insurance (SSDI)
This benefit is for workers who suffer from
impairments which prevent them from working
and is paid for out of the Social Security fund
for retirement. In addition, the surviving spouse
is paid if they have a child 16 or younger or if
the surviving spouse is at least 60 years old or
at least 50 and disabled.

VA Disability
This fund is for disabled veterans and is paid
by income tax dollars. The amount allocated
to the fund is done a year in advance in the
budget to protect against ups and downs.

The VA disability program for fiscal year 2012
and 2013 was established in May of 2012 at a
cost of $148 billion which included a 20%
increase or an additional $10.5 billion in yearly
payments. Payments range from $127 a month
for 10% disability to $2,769 for a 100% one.
In addition to the VA disability and pension
payments, the VA budget allocation also will
include spending for the medical services
provided by the Veterans Administration.

Supplemental Nutrition Assistance (SNAP)

This program formerly known as food stamps is a federal program for low income people administered by the state and local governments and is funded by the general fund from income taxes paid by the workers.

Social Security

This fund is for retirement and is paid for by contributions from the employee and employer. Eligibility is age 65 for those born on or before 1938, age 66 for those born between 1943 and 1954 and age 67 for those born in 1960 or later. Anyone is eligible for early retirement at age 62 and will get a pro-rated lesser amount than if they had waited until the normal retirement age.

The Social Security system is terribly flawed in every aspect. It assumes that the working base will continue to grow as the population grows and the contributions will always exceed monies taken out and that the economy will continue to grow indefinitely.

There are 4 reasons why this fund could never

(26)

be sound the way it is currently operated. First, disability payments (SSDI) are paid out of the fund for people who may have contributed very little or nothing into it. This includes some payments for dependent children and surviving spouses who are elderly.

Secondly, under the government's algorithm, the retirement paid out exceeds what the worker and their employer paid into it. My own parents drew out more in five years than they put into it their whole life. To illustrate further, if a person works for 42 years and earns only a total of $60,000 of taxable wages for all of those years, they and their employer would have paid in $7,440 to Social Security but would draw out $200 a month or a total of $43,200 if they live to be 80 years old. The Social Security system does not work like a normal retirement plan where upon retirement the total paid in plus earned fund investments is the total which someone may withdraw.

Thirdly, the government removes surplus balances and spends it for whatever they wish

and replaces it with IOU's by issuing special bonds and certificates of indebtedness for which interest must be paid. The fund debt as of 2009 was $2.5 trillion and this debit is not counted as part of the national debt since we borrowed it from ourselves and not from an outside source such as China, but when it gets paid back, where will the money come from?

The fourth reason the fund will be short is that upon death of the person receiving social security, their surviving spouse receives a significant prorated share of their benefit even though the surviving spouse may not have ever paid into the system. If Social Security worked like a normal retirement plan there should not be any shortage in the fund at any time. Congress should not be allowed to take funds from this trust fund for any reason, as it belongs to the people who paid into it and are expecting it to be held in trust.

The following are the rates for Social Security and Medicare:

.0145 % Medicare (no wage limit)
.0620 % Soc. Sec. (wage limit of $110,100)
.0765 % Total employee contributions
.0765 % Employer contribution
.1530 % Total Contribution

The employee rate for Social Security for 2011 and 2012 was .0420. This reduction of .0200% is referred to as the "payroll tax holiday" and is a reduction to the employee's social security contributions. The employer rate remained the same at .0620 %. This tax holiday will result in a $185 billion short payment into social security for the years 2011 and 2012.

When employees reach the Social Security maximum at a job during the year and change jobs, their Social Security withholding's continue again thus creating an overpayment for the year but they can claim any excess payments back on their tax return but

(29)

employers don't get any credit and the government keeps their excess money.

The Lower class (0-$30k) and middle class ($31-$120k) pay most of the Social Security whereas the upper class ($120-$250K) and the wealthy ($250+k) pay nothing after their annual limit of $6,826.

When one is considering whether to retire at 62 or their normal retirement age of 65, 66 or 67, they should first find out what their payments would be under either option. One can find out what those numbers are by visiting the Social Security web site or by writing to the Social Security Administration to get the information. Next, make a simple spread sheet which will show you differences, such as this example:

	Mthly Pymt			
Year #.............	1	4	6	15
Age..............	62	65	67	76
Age 62 800	9600	38400	57600	**144000**
Age 65 1000		12000	36000	**144000**
Age 67 1200			14400	**144000**

(30)

This model, which does not include a cost of living allowance, shows that you would not lose anything by retiring at 62 for 15 years.

Even though there was no cost of living given for 2010 and 2011, there normally is a COLA of 1% to 3%, so let's see what the same model would look like if you added a 2% COLA for each year:

	Mthly Pymt				
Year #..............		4........	6........	17.........	18
Age...............		65......	67.......	78.........	79
Age 62	800	39567	60558	192116	205558
Age 65	1000		36725	191687	**207521**
Age 67	1200		14400	**193134**	211397

This model shows that you would not lose any retirement at age 62 compared to retiring at age 65 or 67 until after 17 years or age 78.

All public employees at the local, state and federal level including Congress, should have to contribute to and use the same Social

Security and Medicare systems that people in the private sector use. Cities, Counties and States should have the option to select their own retirement and pension plans in lieu of using the Social Security system if they can get a better fund growth rate but should have strict restrictions on those funds such as not allowing the government entity to borrow or remove any of the funds.

Other entitlement programs
In addition to these federal programs there are many more at the state level some of which are funded by the federal government or the state income taxes or a shared cost between the state and federal governments.

The Government assistance programs averaged $3,686 in 1990, $4,763 in 2000 and $7,427 in 2010 per American citizen per year. 1/2 of the population does not work or pay taxes (minors and students), 1/4 of the population works and pay taxes and 1/4, or 78 million, do not work or pay taxes and receive government entitlements.

(32)

Billions are being wasted on fraud and abuse from federal and state entitlement programs. The following is a first hand account of fraud that I personally witnessed with the IHSS (In Home Support Services) program run by the state of California whereby the state pays a caregiver to care for a person who is dependent and on Medicare and state assistance:

One of my relatives had an elderly aunt who was a widow but had some money in the banks and an annuity which she had not started to withdraw when she met a man at the Senior Center who already had a criminal background and he was on Social Security, Medicare and the IHSS assistance program.

This man started a courtship with her, no doubt after learning she had some money, and in short time forcibly moved in with her. This alerted my relative who was her executor, to start looking into her finances and he discovered large sums of money missing from her bank accounts but at this point the aunt was too

senile to realize what was going on.

My relative returned from a vacation just in time to stop the lecherous man from withdrawing her annuity. He then stopped all action on all of her money accounts but not before the man had ripped off more than $70K of her money.

My relative then learned that the man was receiving IHSS payments to his grandson but the grandson had never provided any services for the man. He also learned that the son had originally received the payments but merely cashed the checks and had never provided any services that are required under the IHSS program.

IHSS was paying the grandson in excess of $1,000 each month for services he did not provide. This went on for approximately six months.

First of all, one wonders how he was able to get the assistance in the first place given he

showed no visible signs of needing care and was not seeing a doctor on any regular basis. All of his bodily functions seemed normal and he was not on any life support medications.

The County case worker is required to check on people who are receiving IHSS support at least once a month to see how they are doing and if they are at risk, to see them more often. My own mother was seen every week and sometimes twice a week. Her caregiver earned every penny he got to care for her. The amount paid to the caregiver is based on what services they provide and can go up or down each month depending on what the IHSS case worker deems necessary.

A county case worker only visited the man twice. Once to get his grandson set up as his caregiver and once to talk to the man about a new housing arrangement.
On the last visit by the case worker, the man broke down and confessed he had stolen some money, but he didn't know what to do. The case worker had no recommendation. When the case

worker was leaving, my relative told him that the district attorney's office was investigating the man for theft. The case worker indicated that was no concern of his and there was nothing he could do. There was never a follow up visit.

Since he stole the money before they were married and then got married afterward, the district attorney could not charge the man for stealing money from his wife unless she stated that he stole the money from her bank accounts. Because of her state of dementia, she could not remember how the money disappeared. So she said she must have given him the money so he would not go to jail. At that point, the district attorney terminated the investigation,

I then got involved to try to get IHSS to get the man for fraud. I first found out the name of his case worker, her supervisor and if all else failed, who to contact at the State level. Fearing that if I started with his case worker, she would not take any action because it would show she was negligent in her duties so I sent an email to her supervisor telling her

(36)

what was going on and that it had been going on for at least three years of which we knew.

I received an answer from the supervisor saying that she would check into it. After two months, I inquired again to see what was going on and she informed me that the allegations had been forwarded to the proper people to investigate. After two more months, I sent my complaint to the State and again received a reply that they would look into it.

I never heard from anyone again and got tired of pursuing it any further but it makes one wonder if the whole system is inept or corrupt, but one thing is certain, and that is, there is a lot of fraud and waste in the system.

In order to clean up Medicare and Medicaid, those functions should be done by the private sector and leave the government to be the enforcer when fraud and abuse is discovered. Rewards should be given the private sector firms who administer the programs to provide them with an incentive to administer the

(37)

programs and weed out those who are cheating the system. This incentive reward could be a fixed amount per occurrence found or an amount equal to 3-6 months of what the fraudulent recipient was receiving and then the guilty person should be charged with a felony, with severe punishment.

There is unchecked fraud and abuse in every government program that exists, resulting in billions and billions of taxpayer dollars wasted. I talked to a 40 year old woman who had been a registered nurse but was sitting on her sofa becoming more and more over weight. She said she was on Federal SSI benefits because her over weight condition did not allow her to work. Additionally, she was on food stamps and every program she could qualify for. She said if those programs didn't exist, she would not have gained the weight and kept working at her profession but since they did, she was going to take advantage of them. She also volunteered that it was something she had learned from others who did the same thing so why should she work when she didn't have to.

(38)

Even though the government employs thousands of people to handle administration and enforcement of the entitlement programs, very little gets done to reduce the fraud in the programs and once a program gets started, it never ends, they just keep growing and taking more and more tax dollars from the working class.

Mortgages & Real Estate

Although the banks were a major contributor in producing the housing crisis, they were not the sole offenders. In an effort to energize the housing market, the federal government imposed mandated regulations requiring the banks to make loans where the borrowers were not qualified. After the crash, the feds blamed the banks as if they did the faulty loans all on their own accord.

The bad housing market was due to a number of different people all motivated by money. The realtors want to push the values as high as possible in order to get higher commissions. The city and county governments want higher prices so their tax revenue will be greater and allow developers into the community to build homes that are two and three times higher than the average homes already there. These officials also get on board with developers when they are promised additional monies for their community infrastructure.

In two adjoining small communities in northern California the local governments allowed developers to come in and build two story homes priced in the range of $280,000 when the average price of homes had been $100,000 and the average family incomes was less than $40,000. As a result, only 10% of the homes sold to retirees from outside the area and a few executives who commuted to the big city to work. The developers could not sell the other 90% of homes even with price reductions and after two years were reducing prices down to $170,000 and still could not sell the homes. If the city officials had used common sense instead of being lured by the promise of larger tax revenues, they should never have allowed the developments to happen. Like wise, the developers and the banks who financed the projects would not have created a large financial problem for themselves.

In the 1980's the average home prices in Arizona were in the upper range of $80k to $100K. At The same time the prices in the

Silicon Valley in California had already doubled, tripled and quadrupled. Intel Corp. decided to open plants in Arizona to take advantage of the lower taxes and lower labor rates and brought thousands of their bay area employees to Arizona which created an immediate demand for homes. The realty community saw a great opportunity and started to raise prices on the existing homes in Arizona because the high-tech immigrants from California found those prices to be a real bargain compared to what their prices were. In rapid fashion the realtors established favorable comparative home sale prices (Comps) and started driving up the real estate prices all over the state. Well, other than the Intel's and the Motorola's, Arizona's economy was primarily still tourism and after a few short years, the real estate market came to an abrupt halt because the average wage earner could not afford the newly established home prices. Home prices topped out and receded over the next ten years but the market was then stable again.

(42)

This should have been a lesson for Arizona but their memories only lasted about 10 years. During last half of the 90's and half way through the 2000 decade the crazed escalation of prices began again, not only in California and Arizona, but all over the country. Without regard to the average income of residents, prices raised in parts of the country that had never seen this before and soon it was beyond control. Bad loans coupled with low wages or no wages and bad economy brought it all crashing down. In the case of Arizona, their real estate prices went down 40% to 60% between 2008 and 2010.

The following is an example of a loan turning bad and a possible solution that may be used which I call the SEM (shared equity mortgage):

Original purchase price $165,000.
Down payment   (15,000.)
Mortgage owed 4/01/2000 @ 6% 150,000.
Monthly payments of $900/month
Principal paid 4/1/00 to 4/1/06   (13,000).
Mortgage balance 4/01/2006   137,000.

Market Value 4/1/06	187,000.
Equity in home	50,000.

Equity taken out and loan refinanced	
at 5% on 4/1/06	30,000.
New Mortgage balance 4/1/06	167,000.
Monthly payments of $975/month	

Principal paid 4/1/06 to 4/1/09	(11,000.)
Mortgage balance 4/1/09	156,000.

Market value 4/1/09	120,000.

Borrower loses job and must take a job at
a lesser amount which means he can now only
afford a payment of $700 which would
require reducing interest rate to 2.5%
or extending loan to 53 years which are not
viable solutions for the lender.

By using a "shared equity mortgage" (SEM),
the borrower would be allowed to pay $700
and the payment difference of $275 a month
would accrue until the house is sold. Two
years later the mortgage balance is $154,750.

(44)

The house sells for $166,750 leaving a surplus of $12,000 but instead of the borrower getting all of the surplus, he would get $5,400 and the lender would retain $6,600 or $275 a month for 24 months. If the proceeds are less than $6,600 the lender could agree to accept that amount and the borrower would get nothing.

This approach would keep the lender from foreclosing when a borrower can no longer make their payments, provide an alternative for the homeowner to remain in the home and give the lender future equity in the home.

Federal Balanced Budget

The mentality of government entities seems to be to spend whatever they want without regard to whether the revenues are there to support it. If they go over budget they want to raise the taxes on the taxpayers or get a subsidy or grant from the next higher level of government. This practice has created a dependency chain from local government to County to State to the Federal level. Even though some states use a balanced budget, if they go over, they will go to the Feds for help.

Even though the federal budget deals with large numbers and uses a lot of estimates for their projections of revenue and expenses, the budgeting concept is as simple as the one a family would use at their kitchen table. What will the revenue be, how much expense do we have to pay and what, if anything, is left over?

The federal government can only raise taxes, or borrow the money. They currently borrow 42 cents of every dollar spent. The interest

alone is the third largest item in the budget behind military and entitlement spending. This is like someone with a personal credit card who just keeps charging, the interest keeps getting higher until they can afford only the interest and never cut into the principal or in this case, the national debt.

An amendment to the constitution is required to put in a balanced budget at the federal level. To effect this, a constitutional convention will be required. Two-thirds or 34 of the states must call for the convention and thus far 28 of the states have called for the convention. Once proposed, the balanced budget amendment must then be ratified by three-fourths or a minimum of 38 states to take effect. The American people overwhelmingly support this but the politicians do not want the constraints it would bring on their spending.

A balanced budget amendment is needed to control the runaway congressional spending. After establishing a base-line budget, the following years' budgets should be the lesser

of 3% increase over last years' budget or 18% of GDP. That will hold the budgets more in line with the current economy and prevent runaway increases in budgets.

The budget should be completed and passed no later than 5 days prior to the beginning of the new fiscal year. The deadline should not be extended by continuing resolution and for every day the budget is not passed beyond the deadline, every member of congress should forfeit their pay without any future reimbursement.
Exceptions to budget over spending should be limited to a declaration of war, as approved by Congress, natural disaster assistance and extraordinary terrorist activities.

Nearly every politician will say they support a balanced budget when they are behind the microphone, but the reality is the politicians do not want the restriction of a balanced budget, so it is going to take the taxpayers to to be aggressive about it and put the pressure on our Senators and Representatives.

State & Local Union Contracts

The practice of Governors and Mayors negotiating union contracts for public employees and teachers is the biggest threat to the integrity of the public sector. The rash of city and state governments facing bankruptcy across America from 2008 through 2012 is proof that union contracts were approved which favored the union demands without regard to whether there would be enough revenue coming in to meet the demand.

Again, this practice is an open invitation for corruption. Union promises of political contributions to the officials will always get them a favorable contract.

A bipartisan committee composed of 2 Democrats, 2 Republicans, 1 Independent, 1 CPA financial expert and the Mayor, County Supervisor or Governor should comprise the makeup of the budget committee for local and state budgets. After the budget committee has agreed to a budget, it should

(49)

then be submitted to the city council, the board of supervisors or the state legislature to get a final review before it takes effect.

In simple terms, a public entity should operate the same as we individuals do and not spend more than we have available to spend.

The revenue forecast should be based on the prior years' revenue plus any new additional known tax increases. Conversely, it should be reduced by any lowering of tax rates for the next fiscal year. This may be an over simplification of the revenue forecast but a realistic forecast should be done first. This number represents all that is available to be spent.

The compilation of a sound budget for any city, county or state should not require rocket science. The next step in building a budget should be to identify the fixed recurring expenses not including personnel costs plus any known new expenses that will become due in the next year.

(50)

The revenue minus the fixed expenses will represent what can be spent on salaries and the retirement benefits.

First, public sector salaries should not be greater than those in the private sector. The establishment of wage scales should be done on a local basis and not compared to some other state or national average or a small rural area compared to a big city in the same state. There are several companies which provide private sector wage ranges for all job classifications by area or region which can be used to establish comparable wage scales in the private sector.

Public sector retirement plans should not exceed what is employed in the private sector and should work like a 401k or annuity plan. The monthly retirement pay should never be higher than the working wage monthly amount yet we hear of examples all the time where a public sector retired person is receiving more per month than they were as an active employee.

(51)

For budgeting purposes, the current salaries per month (without raises) should be annualized. This should be reduced by estimated retirements based on prior years' average retirements for those who will attain retirement age in the coming fiscal year.

Next, the estimated retirees plus those already on retirement can be added together along with their benefits to arrive at the total forecast for the next year.

The annualized salary forecast plus the retirement benefit forecast will be the total personnel forecast for the next fiscal year. That number then can be compared to the available monies that can be spent (revenue minus fixed costs) and if the personnel costs are greater than the money available, something must be reduced in order to get a balanced budget. Either the employee contributions must be increased or benefits reduced or salaries frozen or reduced or employees laid off. Only if there is a surplus after deducting the personnel costs should

(52)

any raises be considered.

To arrive at a union contract, it should not be for more than three years at a time in case some unknown factors come into play which could put the public entity in a deficit situation.

Privatizing Government Functions

As many services as possible should be contracted to the private sector with the exception of police and fire and then in some cases that can be done as well, by contracting services from a nearby town or from the county.

The city of Sandy Springs, Georgia did just that, which created competition for services which resulted in better service for a much lesser price.

This community of 90,000 people only employed police and fire and avoided the costs of full time employees with high costs of pensions and benefits and also eliminated the "political" environment" which comes with city funded services and unions.

Sandy Springs has a total of 196 employees including the police and fire whereas the nearby city of Roswell with a population of around 85,000, has 1,400 employees and a

budget of over $30 million more than Sandy Springs.

For the cost of 4 public employees, you can employ 5-6 private sector employees due to the public sectors' higher wage scale and benefits. Therefore, privatizing government functions can be a positive thing for the private sector and save the tax payers money and get more for each dollar spent.

Outsourcing can begin by doing a cost-benefit analysis of the services to be considered done to see if the private sector can perform the services cheaper and better than with staffing by the government entity. In a lot of small towns, they do not have the expertise to do an accurate analysis so that task should be done by a third party qualified to do so.

The adage that the lowest bid is best for the government entity should not be used. Anyone can bid lower than someone else but that does not guarantee that the service will be the best for the government. Other factors such as the

(55)

bidders' length of time in business, whether they are insured and bond-able, and of course their references need to be thoroughly checked.

Opponents of privatization argue that the provider may cut corners in order to maximize their profits or that "politics" may enter into the selection of the outsourcing. Correctly done and with the proper oversight and review, competition can bring prices down. The outsources have a tremendous incentive to perform, as they would lose the future business or any re-bids.

In the last 30 years many local, county and state governments have saved millions of dollars by hiring outside contractors or by using neighboring city's services for things like waste management, water treatment and road repair.

If government entities, especially the small ones, would use outsourcing, they could save a lot of money. If the government officials

would look at their entity as a private sector company does and insure their costs are as low as possible, they would be better served and keep their taxpayer's tax rates as low as possible.

It seems as though government officials look at their revenue projections and then decide how they will spend "all" of it. There seems to be a mentality that the next years' budget must not be lower than the current year or they will never be able to justify their tax rates. How about lowering the costs as much as possible, then if there is a surplus, lower the tax rates and rates for utilities and services for the taxpayers?

Prison Farms

Billions of dollars are spent on prisons and the prisoners sit around and watch television and do not acquire any skills they can use if they get out.

Prison farms were tried in Arizona in the 70's with great success but were shut down when the private sector complained that the prison products which were being sold to the general public were selling for far less than they were charging, creating unfair trade subsidized by the government. Some other states who tried utilizing prison farms were shut down due to political pressure, saying that the use of the prisoners for labor, was akin to slavery for the prison black population.

Many states use prison farms to supply eggs, milk, grits, fruits, vegetables, beef, poultry, grains, lumber, clothing and even do some manufacturing. These products supply the prisons in their state and some sell their excess to other states. The prisoners get a stipend

wage ranging from 40 to 90 cents an hour.

Prisoners learn trade skills such as agriculture, crop raising and rotation, food processing, equipment operation, repair and maintenance, computer skills, carpentry, plumbing, etc. By doing a days' work, they develop better social skills and a better sense of self worth.

The most successful prison farms are done by the state of South Carolina. They report they produce three nutritious meals a day for a cost of only $1.51 serving the state's 24,000 prison inmates and save the taxpayers over $400,000 a year.

The total of inmates working the prison farms totals over 35,000 for all states with the state of Arkansas employing the most inmates with a total of 5,200 which is 40% of their total state prison population and 15% of the total of all states' working inmates. Inmates are signing up on the waiting list to be used in the prison farms. Farming produces rehabilitation and therapy through working with and caring

for plants and animals.

Prison farms should be expanded in all states to supply their own state prisons as much as possible but also to supply the government outlets where welfare recipients only, could shop for food, clothing, furniture, etc. using their allotted welfare scripts. (See chapter on using Government stores).

The people on welfare would no longer be able to shop at regular retail outlets saving the taxpayers billions of dollars. It would also give welfare recipients an incentive to get off the welfare and back into the normal flows of society.

The government could also use the prisoners to do copying, printing and mailings which would reduce the governments' clerical costs.

In summary, we could utilize the idle hands and minds of the prison population to supply the prisons with their needs and secondarily supply the people on food stamps without the

taxpayers having to subsidize the entitlement
community.

Government Stores

The concept of having government stores for the recipients of food stamps may seem far fetched and unimaginable but consider the plausible merits of implementing it.

In the past four years the Food Stamp program (known as the SNAP - Supplemental Nutrition Assistance Program) increased 135 percent to reach a cost of $78 billion in 2011. In the same four year period, the number of Americans on food stamps has increased by 70 percent to 45 million recipients or one out of every seven U.S. residents who received benefits each month during 2011. The CBO estimates that the program will continue to grow through 2014.

Instead of giving people food stamps, the government could use grocery stores operated by private sector contractors who have the retail experience to do so.

Literally billions of dollars would be saved

and the people on the entitlement would have an incentive to get off the program if they wanted to get back into the mainstream of society where they can earn a wage and shop anywhere they choose.

The suppliers to these government stores should be the local farmers, the prison farms (see chapter on prison farms) and then the normal wholesalers who supply the private sector retail stores.

First priority for meats and vegetables should be directly from the local farmers, if present in the area. The farmers could then get a higher price for their products than they would from from their co-op or wholesaler and the store would get a lower price as well.

The second priority source should be from the the prison farms. This would be the lowest price for food products even though there may be transportation and storage costs involved.

Everything else to stock a retail market would

have to come from the private sector wholesalers. With a nationwide chain of Government stores, a good price could be negotiated for all products required.